Cornerstones of Freedom

The Roaring Twenties

R. Conrad Stein

CHILDRENS PRESS®

CHICAGO

Library of Congress Cataloging-in-Publication Data

Stein, R. Conrad.
    The roaring twenties / by R. Conrad Stein.
       p. cm. – (Cornerstones of freedom)
    ISBN 0-516-06675-7
    1. United States–History–1919-1933–Juvenile literature.
    I. Title. II. Series.
E784.S69 1994   93-37029
973.91–dc20   CIP
                                               AC

It was one of the wildest decades in American history. The Roaring Twenties, the period between 1920 and 1930, began with the hope of world peace and ended with the fear of economic ruin. In between, Americans discarded traditions and rewrote old rules. Novelist F. Scott Fitzgerald said of the 1920s, "The parties were bigger . . . the pace was faster . . . the morals were looser and the liquor was cheaper."

In the summer of 1919, long parades of soldiers returning from World War I wound down main streets while bands played "When Johnny Comes Marching Home." The war had brought fear and uncertainty to the land. Now Americans longed to go back to their normal, pre-war routines. Politicians promised the nation "a return to normalcy." However, the 1920s proved to be anything but a normal era.

The first remarkable change of the new decade was the closing of all the nation's saloons. Prohibition, the forbidding of alcoholic drinks, was the dominant issue of the 1920s. For decades, churches and women's groups had sought to ban alcohol, insisting that drinking was destroying the minds and bodies of American men. World War I renewed their demands, as

A government agent closing down a tavern during Prohibition

3

A hidden entry to a speakeasy

prohibition advocates argued that the grain processed to make beer and liquor could be better used to feed people in lands ravaged by warfare. Many prohibitionists wore badges proclaiming BREAD, NOT BOOZE. By 1919, the voters in three-fourths of the American states had approved the Eighteenth Amendment to the U.S. Constitution, which forbade the import, sale, or manufacture of alcoholic beverages. Throughout the 1920s, Prohibition was the law of the land.

No ordinance in American history was so openly violated as was Prohibition. All levels of American society rebelled against the ban on alcohol. Within six months after Prohibition began, thousands of secret illegal taverns—called

After years of demonstrations and growing public support, Prohibition became national law in 1919.

Although federal agents were dogged in their efforts to find and destroy alcohol, people still found ways to sneak the illegal stuff.

speakeasies—had sprung up all over the land. In the mid-1920s, the New York City chief of police estimated that 32,000 "speaks" operated in his city alone. A secret knock and hushed words such as "Tommy sent me" admitted a customer to a speakeasy. The better places sold booze smuggled across the border from Canada, or beer made in clandestine breweries. Speakeasies that catered to the poor offered foul-smelling green beer and liquor laced with industrial-strength alcohol to provide a kick.

Prohibition was only one of the new phenomena ushered in by the new decade.

Americans of the time were dazzled by an array of newly developed gadgets and inventions. The phrase "What will they think of next?" was coined in the 1920s.

In 1919, only one-third of American homes had electricity; by 1929, that figure had climbed to two-thirds. To people accustomed to lighting their houses with candles or smoky gas lamps, modern electric lightbulbs seemed miraculous. Electricity was so new and so little understood by the public that drugstores of the 1920s sold special caps to put over electric outlets. People

During the 1920s, rising prosperity and the use of credit prompted Americans to buy gadgets and appliances like never before.

Listening to the radio became the most popular form of home entertainment in the 1920s.

believed that without the caps, the electricity would spill out onto the floor.

Almost overnight, radio was transformed from scratchy crystal sets listened to only by hobbyists to the highlight of family entertainment. The first commercial radio station was Pittsburgh's KDKA, which began broadcasting in 1920. By the end of the decade, more than six hundred radio stations were in business. Ornate radio receivers with horn-like speakers became centerpieces in American parlors, much the way television sets are today. Singers such as Rudy Vallee and Jessica Dragonette were the raves of 1920s radio.

Rudy Vallee

The popular, affordable Model T Ford rolls down the assembly line.

The single device that produced the decade's most revolutionary change was the automobile. A generation earlier, automobiles were playthings for the rich. But mass production drove the prices down, and by the 1920s, anyone with a decent job could aspire to own a "gas buggy." American families viewed them as four-wheeled dreams. When a farm housewife was asked why she chose to buy a car even though the family did not own a bathtub, she answered, "Because you can't drive to town in a bathtub."

By 1929, 23 million cars jammed American roads, triple the number of nine years earlier. Almost half a million Americans worked in auto-manufacturing plants. King of the industry was the Ford Motor Company of Detroit. In 1908,

Henry Ford had introduced a simple, reliable car he called the Model T. It had a twenty-horsepower engine, which gave it a top speed of forty miles per hour. Early models cost $850. By increasing the efficiency of his assembly lines, Ford brought the price down to $290 in 1924. By 1927, some 15 million Model T's had been produced, and the American way of life was changed forever. Humorist and folk philosopher Will Rogers said, "Good luck, Mr. Ford. It will take a hundred years to tell whether you have helped us or hurt us, but you certainly didn't leave us like you found us."

Henry Ford in his first car, built in 1896

Vacationers' cars jam Nantucket Beach, Massachusetts, in 1925.

Sheet music to
a popular 1920s
dance tune

A social revolution took place among the young people of the 1920s, who one writer nicknamed the "Flaming Youth." Members of the Flaming Youth lived for pleasure. Their music was fast-paced and their gyrating dances, such as the Charleston, shocked the older generation. A columnist for a Cincinnati newspaper attended a college dance and reported, "The music is sensuous, the embracing of partners absolutely indecent, and the motions may not be described in a family newspaper." Young men and women created their own language. "You're the cat's meow" meant "you're wonderful"; "You're a flat tire" meant "you're dull and boring."

Photographs and cartoons from the era captured the new wild behavior of the nation's young people.

Flagpole sitting and playing tennis atop a soaring airplane were among the zany antics attempted by thrill seekers in the 1920s.

Fads and zany antics were a passion with the Flaming Youth, and even among the older crowd. A newspaper in Warsaw, Indiana, reported, "Clarence Tillman, 17, local high school student, put 40 sticks of chewing gum in his mouth at one time, sang 'Home Sweet Home,' and between verses of the song drank a gallon of milk." Flagpole sitting was the rage. The record-holding flagpole sitter was an ex-boxer named Alvin "Shipwreck" Kelly, who sat perched atop a flagpole in Baltimore for twenty-three days and seven hours. Food and drink were hoisted up to him. Kelly paid a man on the ground to scream and wake him up whenever it seemed he were about to doze off.

Flappers showing off their bold new fashions

A woman having her hair "bobbed"

Young women led the youth madness by dressing in a fashion that outraged their mothers. Just a few years earlier, a properly attired lady wore a dress that hugged her neck and flowed down to her ankles. During the twenties, necklines plunged and hemlines rose to reveal a woman's knees. Women who dressed in such a shocking manner were called flappers, a British term originally describing a baby bird emerging from its nest with wildly flapping wings. Flappers further defied authority by bobbing their hair (cutting it boyishly short), using lipstick, and rolling their stockings down to their knees. Some people considered the flappers' form of dress to be little short of nudity. In Utah, angry legislators introduced a law banning "skirts higher than three inches above the ankle."

Historians and sociologists argue about what caused the change in American manners and morals during the 1920s. Some say that Americans were simply breathing a collective sigh of relief now that the difficult years of World War I were over. Young men and women were anxious to put wartime discipline and hardship behind them and enjoy life to its fullest.

Prosperity and an increase in leisure time also fueled the decade-long party. Middle-class Americans had never had it so good. The expanding electrical and auto industries provided jobs. Industrial production in the United States climbed 50 percent between 1920 and 1929.

Magazine ads of the 1920s played on the general mood of prosperity to sell everything from salad dressing to lightbulbs.

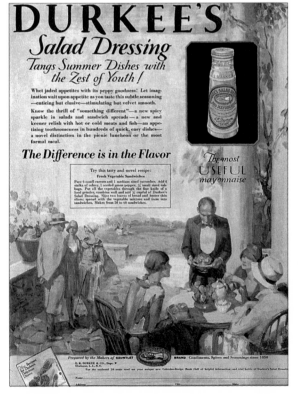

A busy stockbroker's office during the 1920s stock boom

People had money in the bank, and many families put their spare dollars in the stock market.

The stock market is a time-honored capitalistic institution. Through the market, corporations raise money by selling shares of their worth in the form of stocks. The stocks fluctuate in price, depending on how many people are willing to buy them. During the 1920s, millions of eager buyers bought shares in the stock market. And why not? Between 1920 and 1926, the average price per share on the New York Stock Exchange increased 62 percent. In the year 1928 alone, a share of Radio Corporation of America zoomed from $85 to $420. Anyone who had bought RCA shares when the price was low could make thousands of dollars by selling them after the price shot up. Writer F. Scott Fitzgerald claimed he went to get a haircut from his favorite New York barber, and was told the man had retired because he recently earned half a million on the stock market.

Certainly not everyone shared in the prosperity of the 1920s. African Americans, recent immigrants, and farmers were among those who were largely untouched by the good times. For blacks in the South, economic conditions had changed little since slavery. Most southern blacks worked as sharecroppers, and had to give up as much as 75 percent of the crops they raised to

Southern sharecroppers were among those who were untouched by the nationwide prosperity of the 1920s.

Even in the 1920s, many immigrants who had settled in American cities still worked long hours for little pay in crowded, dirty "sweatshops."

their white landlords. The millions of immigrants who had come to America from southern and eastern Europe early in the century continued living in grim big-city neighborhoods, wondering when they could claim their share of New World riches. Farmers enjoyed prosperity during World War I when crop prices soared, but prices for farm goods plunged after the war and never regained their wartime highs.

If immigrants or African Americans complained about their conditions, they risked being attacked by the Ku Klux Klan. This white-supremacist group was anti-black, anti-Catholic, anti-Jewish, and anti-foreigner. The organization reached the peak of its power in the mid-1920s, when its membership grew to more than 4 million and included powerful politicians and law enforcement officers.

Nor was its influence confined to the South. In the North, job competition from immigrants and blacks who had migrated from the South triggered old hatreds and helped swell the Klan's ranks. The Grand Dragon (leader) of the Indiana branch of the Klan, D. C. Stephenson, had such great political backing that he was able to say, "I am the law in Indiana." In terrible sprees of violence called "night rides," white-hooded Klan members stormed through farm regions lynching, whipping, and terrorizing people. Their

The Ku Klux Klan, here marching in Washington, D.C., in 1925, reached the peak of its popularity in the 1920s.

victims might include an outspoken African American, or a white preacher who dared to say from the pulpit that blacks and whites were equal in the eyes of God.

By 1925, interest in the KKK began to decline. The group's plunge in popularity was hastened when Klan leader D.C. Stephenson was convicted of murdering his girlfriend. The details of the murder were so bizarre that the reputation of the entire organization was tarnished.

America's most talented writers often felt alienated by 1920s society and the injustices and frivolous behavior they saw around them. Sinclair Lewis's powerful novel *Main Street* was a

Writers Sinclair Lewis (left) and F. Scott Fitzgerald (right)

Ernest Hemingway and his second wife, Pauline

sharp satire of pettiness and prejudice in a small American town. F. Scott Fitzgerald won readers among the Flaming Youth because his characters delighted in breaking the rules. A young lady in Fitzgerald's novel *This Side of Paradise* says, "I'm just full of the devil." Writers such as Gertrude Stein and Ernest Hemingway fled to Paris in the 1920s. There they formed a literary circle composed of Americans who had suffered through World War I and were now dismayed by the post-war world. Gertrude Stein told her American friends living abroad, "You are all a lost generation." From then on, the angry writers of the 1920s were referred to as the Lost Generation.

Gertrude Stein

King Oliver's Creole Jazz Band

Perhaps the most lasting art form to emerge in the Roaring Twenties was that uniquely American style of music known as jazz. In fact, another nickname for the 1920s is the Jazz Age. An outgrowth of ragtime, blues, and black spiritual music, jazz drifted out of the South and found devoted fans in northern cities. Black musicians were the inventors of jazz. The greatest group of the decade was King Oliver's Creole Jazz Band, which performed to large audiences on Chicago's South Side. The band's leading player was Louis Armstrong, a New

Orleans-born trumpeter who later became jazz music's most famous ambassador.

Sports heroes dominated the headlines of the time. Yankees slugger Babe Ruth was idolized for his home-run hitting and for the casual way he earned and spent money. Ruth was once chided about the fact that he made more in one year than did the president of the United States. "Well," said Ruth, "I had a better year." Football's most illustrious player was Red Grange, the swift halfback from the University of Illinois. Writer Damon Runyon described Grange's elusive style of running as "melody and symphony."

Babe Ruth (left) and Red Grange (right) both enjoyed glory years in the 1920s.

The fight of the decade: Jack Dempsey (standing) vs. Gene Tunney

Greta Garbo

Streets in big cities and small towns were unusually quiet on the night of September 22, 1927, as Americans listened on their radios to the fight of the decade: the heavyweight match between Jack Dempsey and Gene Tunney. Dempsey lost, and when his wife asked him what had happened in the ring, he answered simply, "Honey, I forgot to duck."

Top movie stars of the 1920s received up to 30 million letters each year from adoring fans.

*Rudolph
Valentino was
the most popular
romantic movie
star of the 1920s.*

The beautiful Greta Garbo was known to be vain
and standoffish, but those traits somehow added
to her allure. Flappers swooned over Rudolph
Valentino, whose most famous role was that of a
dashing desert prince in *The Sheik*. A top hat, a
cane, and a herky-jerky walk were the trademark
of Charlie Chaplin, the decade's great comedy
star. Silent movies prevailed through most of the
1920s, but in 1927, the first major "talkie" was
released. The addition of sound made movies
even more popular, and film stars continued to
be giants in the hearts of the public.

   The most fabled hero in this hero-worshipping
decade was a shy young aviator named Charles
Lindbergh. On May 20, 1927, Lindbergh took off

Charlie Chaplin

Charles Lindbergh became a hero after he made the first solo, nonstop flight across the Atlantic in 1927.

from an airfield in Long Island, New York, and steered his tiny one-engine aircraft toward the vast Atlantic Ocean. Thirty-three and one-half hours later he landed in Paris, becoming the first person to make a solo, nonstop flight across the Atlantic. New York City welcomed him home with the wildest ticker-tape parade ever seen. Flappers created a new dance—the Lindy—in his honor. But tragedy struck the Lindbergh family.

Five years after the flight, Lindbergh's twenty-month-old son was kidnapped and later found murdered. Brazen newspaper reporters hounded Lindbergh and his wife for details about the crime. A disgusted Charles Lindbergh wrote, "I've had enough fame for a dozen lives. It's not what it's cracked up to be."

Gangsters who defied Prohibition laws controlled America's urban underworld during the Roaring Twenties. King of the beer barons was Chicago's Al Capone. Operating distilleries, breweries, and a string of speakeasies, Capone became a multimillionaire. He used his fortune to control Chicago politicians and police officers. "Everybody calls me a racketeer. I call myself a businessman," Capone once said. "I make my money by supplying a popular demand."

Al Capone was the nation's most notorious gangster in the 1920s.

Capone commanded an army of seven hundred gunmen who waged war with rival gangs trying to cut into his illegal booze operations. One by one, Capone's rivals died violent deaths. On February 14, 1929—St. Valentine's Day— Capone's men gunned down six members of the Bugs Moran gang and a bystander in a Chicago garage. The mass murder was so grisly that even people who had grudgingly admired Capone now condemned him as a mad-dog killer. Because Capone wielded so much power in Chicago, it was nearly impossible to pin any crimes on him. But shortly after the St. Valentine's Day

Hundreds of people line the streets during the funeral procession of a murdered Chicago gangster. In the Roaring Twenties, local crime figures often held more power and influence than local politicians.

Massacre, the federal government finally nabbed him and sent him to prison—for income-tax evasion.

Politics in the 1920s were tumultuous but predictable, as voters sent one Republican president after another to the White House. The first of the long string of Republicans was Warren Harding, elected in November 1920. It was the first presidential election in which women were allowed to vote. Formerly a small-town newspaper owner, Harding seemed overwhelmed by the demands of his office. "Oftentimes I sit here, I don't seem to grasp that I am president," he once confided to a reporter. Harding died on August 2, 1923. After his death, the public learned that some of the president's friends had been helping themselves to government money. Biggest of the crooks was Secretary of the Interior Albert Fall, who went to prison over a moneymaking scheme called the Teapot Dome affair.

Calvin Coolidge became president after Harding's death. He was a rare politician in that he disliked making long speeches. This earned

In 1920, with the passage of the Nineteenth Amendment, woman suffrage (the right to vote) became law throughout the United States.

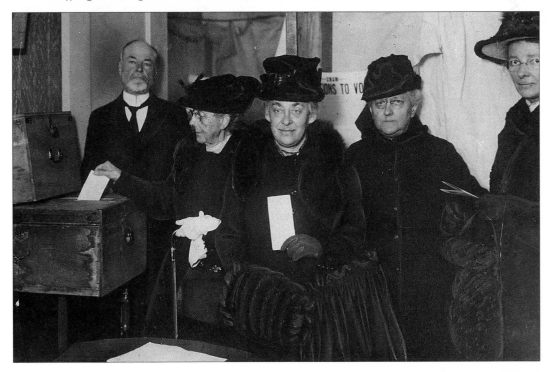

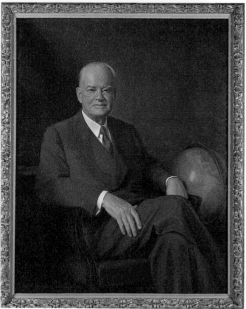

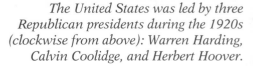

The United States was led by three Republican presidents during the 1920s (clockwise from above): Warren Harding, Calvin Coolidge, and Herbert Hoover.

him the nickname "Silent Cal." He believed in giving free rein to big business, because business interests were seemingly behind the dizzying prosperity the country was enjoying. At the end of his term, Coolidge declared, "I do not choose to run for president in 1928." A humorist said that this simple statement might have been the longest speech Silent Cal gave during his years in office. Herbert Hoover, another Republican, was elected president after Coolidge. The American people later blamed Hoover when the booming economy suddenly went bust.

Throughout the decade, the stock market was a fountain of wealth. The price of most stocks went steadily upward, meaning that putting money in the stock market was like betting on a horse race in which most of the horses were sure winners. In the fall of 1929, however, prices on the stock market began to drop when worried investors who had bought stock on credit began to sell. Panic seized investors on Thursday, October 24, 1929. On that day, known ever after as Black Thursday, falling stock prices spurred an incredible flurry of selling—which in turn caused prices to plummet even more. Black Thursday was followed by Terrifying Tuesday, when so many shares were unloaded that the market collapsed completely.

The stock market crash immediately affected almost everybody—not just those who had invested in it. Most American families kept their savings in banks. Many banks had invested their clients' funds in the stock market. When the market crashed, the banks had nothing to give their clients. In one mind-numbing week, the fortunes of rich people and the life savings of poor and middle-class families were wiped out. It was the worst financial disaster in history.

The stock market crash ended the great party that was the 1920s. The good times had been fueled by confidence that America would remain prosperous forever. By New Year's Eve, 1929, that confidence had vanished. No one yet realized the miseries in store for the nation in the 1930s, the decade of the Great Depression. But the excitement that had charged America for ten dynamic years was missing at New Year's Eve celebrations.

Even though the party was over, memories of it lingered. Years later, when members of an older generation heard once-popular dance numbers such as "Lucky Lindy" or "Ain't We Got Fun?",

Charleston dancers in St. Louis in 1925

they thought back to an era when laughter seemed to rule the country. Aging flappers might recall a poem, written by Edna St. Vincent Millay, that summed up the "live for the moment" spirit of the Roaring Twenties:

> My candle burns at both ends;
> It will not last the night;
> But ah, my foes, and oh, my friends-
> It gives a lovely light!

INDEX

PHOTO CREDITS

Picture Identifications:
Cover: A 1920s magazine cover illustration by John Held, Jr., a famous cartoonist who captured the style and spirit of the flapper era
Page 1: A photo showing clothing and automobile styles of the Roaring Twenties
Page 2: New York City celebrates the end of World War I in November 1918

Project Editor: Shari Joffe
Design: Karen Yops
Photo Research: Jan Izzo
Cornerstones of Freedom Logo: David Cunningham

ABOUT THE AUTHOR

R. Conrad Stein was born and raised in Chicago. He enlisted in the Marine Corps at the age of eighteen and served for three years. He then attended the University of Illinois, where he received a bachelor's degree in history. He later studied in Mexico, earning an advanced degree from the University of Guanajuato. Mr. Stein is the author of many books, articles, and short stories for young people.

Mr. Stein lives in Chicago with his wife and their daughter Janna.